Eagle Eyes

A CHILD'S GUIDE TO PAYING ATTENTION

Eagle Eyes

A CHILD'S GUIDE TO PAYING ATTENTION

BY JEANNE GEHRET, M.A.
Illustrations and design by Susan Covert

Verbal Images Press
Fairport, New York

Many thanks to those who reviewed and consulted on this book:

Cheryl Guenther, parent, The Norman Howard School, New York; **Corinne Olson,** student, New York; **Harvey Parker, Ph.D.,** founder of Children with Attention Deficit Disorders (CH.A.D.D.), Florida; **Jon Price, M.D., F.A.A.P.,** pediatrician, Ohio; **Peg Schoenfeld,** special education teacher, New York; **John F. Taylor, Ph.D.,** family psychologist, Oregon

Special thanks to **Judy Olson,** board member of the Greater Rochester Attention Deficit Disorder Association (GRADDA), who asked for *Eagle Eyes* to be written; and to the naturalists at the Cumming Nature Center of the Rochester Museum and Science Center.

ISBN 0-9625136-4-4 softcover
ISBN 0-9625136-5-2 hardcover
Second edition, second printing
Printed in Mexico

Publisher's Cataloging-in-Publication Data
Gehret, Jeanne.
  Eagle eyes : a child's guide to paying attention / by Jeanne Gehret ; illustrations and design by Susan Covert
  p. cm.
  Includes bibliographical references.
  SUMMARY: Like a river overflowing its banks, Ben wreaks havoc until he learns to recognize and control his attention deficit disorder.
  ISBN 0-9625136-4-4(pbk.)
  ISBN 0-9625136-5-2(hbk.)
  1. Attention deficit disorders--Juvenile literature. I. Title. II. Title: A child's guide to paying attention.
  RJ496.A86G4 1991   153.1532   QBI91-1854

Verbal Images Press
19 Fox Hill Drive • Fairport, New York 14450
(716) 377-3807 • Fax (716) 377-5401

To Eagle Eyes and Emily:
I'm glad for who you are—J.G.

To Richard, who plants the seeds
and waits for the harvest—S.C.

When my family goes to Birdsong Trail, I spot more wildlife than anybody else. Our last couple trips there didn't go so well, though. Here's what happened.

We took birdseed because the chickadees are so tame that they eat right out of people's hands. As soon as I saw the hungry gray birds, I dropped some food on the path. "Ben, stop it," Emily snapped. "If you drop it on the path they won't eat out of our hands." Why didn't I think of that?

As we hiked along the snowy path near the pond, my eyes followed a chickadee to the top of an oak. I spied a clump of leaves and sticks — a nest? An eagle circled high overhead. Suddenly it swooped down into the water and grabbed a fish.

I ran on ahead to where Emily was feeding chickadees. "Emily, guess what," I panted. "I saw an eagle's nest and..." In my haste I tripped, scattering seed on the path. The chickadees flew away from my sister and gathered at my feet, eating greedily.

"You klutz!" she cried. "Can't you ever be quiet? You scared the birds away from me...and now they're all eating at your feet!"

Crying, she turned to Mom and Dad. "I can't have any fun when Ben's around. He's such a pain!" I threw some snow at her.

"Ben, stop!" Mom said. "Would you please be more careful not to scare the birds? Come on, Emily; we'll find other chickadees around the bend."

A pain, I thought—that's me. Always ruining things, making people mad. I stayed behind, thinking, *They're better off without me.*

I walked so slowly that I must have examined every inch of that trail—the bird feeder where cardinals feast, the deer footprints by the bridge, the signpost with the eagle painted on it. I wanted to tell Emily what I saw, but she was still mad. She glared at me all the way home.

After supper Mom said, "Time for homework, kids. Go get your folders and let's see what you have to do."

Emily spoke up quickly. "I don't have any. I finished mine in school on Friday."

"Good job, honey. How about you, Ben?"

"I don't have any either," I replied. But a few minutes later she returned holding a note from my folder. Frowning, she read, "Benjamin has not done his homework for two days. Please have him complete pages 67-75 of these worksheets."

So I had to sit and work the rest of the evening while Emily got to rearrange her fish tank. I was so angry I couldn't fall asleep until midnight.

"Pass your homework in, class," my teacher said the next morning. I smiled to myself, glad that I had mine in my folder for a change. But no, my folder was empty! After all that work!

Shortly after that, Dad took me to see Dr. Lawson. She told me I have Attention Deficit Disorder, which is often called ADD for short. ADD means that my body doesn't have enough of the chemicals that help me control how I move and think. I forget to take my homework to school because my thoughts run ahead of me. That's why I bump into things, too. And all that energy keeps me awake into the night.

All this time I thought I was nothing but a clumsy, bad kid. Huh!

Dad explained that I have eagle eyes; I notice every-thing. But eagles know when to stop looking around and zoom in on their prey. Me, I just keep noticing more things and miss my catch.

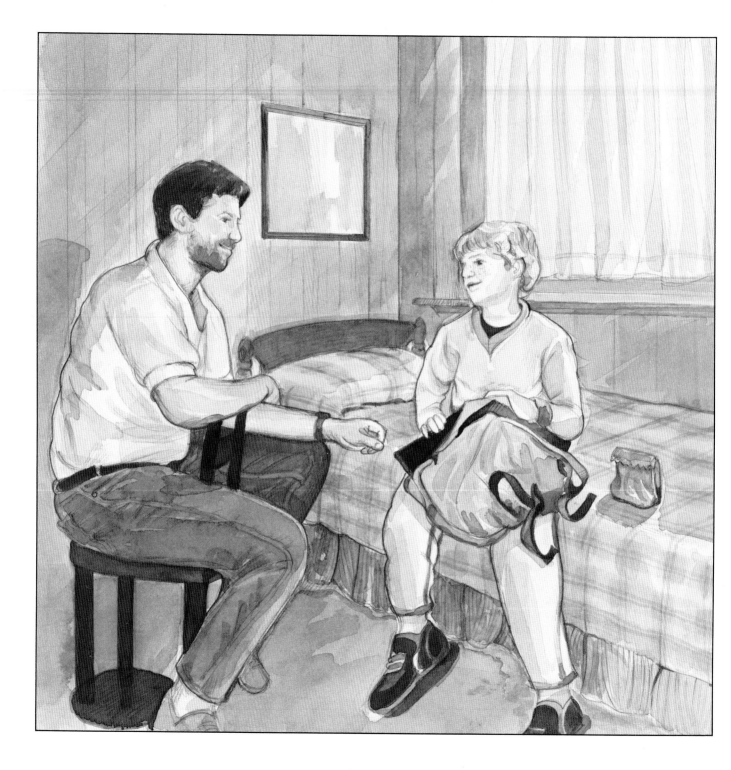

Dr. Lawson showed Dad and me some tricks so I can pay attention to what's important. That night we made up a song about getting ready for school so I'll have everything I need. Here's how it goes:

The Morning Song

adapted from the traditional tune "Oats, peas, beans, and barley"

1. Clothes, hair, shoes, and backpack, lunch, Clothes, hair, shoes and
2. Clear the ta- ble wash my face, Get my coat and

1. backpack, lunch, Clothes, hair, shoes and backpack, lunch, That is what I do.
2. get my boots, Grab my backpack, give a kiss, That is what I do.

When I sing "backpack," I know it's time to put my homework in my backpack. Since I've started singing the Morning Song, I haven't forgotten any of my school things.

Another thing I like is the soft music that Mom gave me to help me relax at night. It quiets the thoughts that run around inside my head. Dr. Lawson prescribed medicine that gives my body more of the chemicals it needs.

Dr. Lawson also taught us to play the Feelings Game. Dad makes a face like he's angry, or sad, or pleased, and I guess how he's feeling by reading his face and body. One day, when I was crayoning on Emily's homework, I noticed that her face looked like Daddy's does when he's mad. I stopped right away and she didn't go crying to Mom like she usually does.

Since we've been doing the things Dr. Lawson suggested, I feel better. And I don't feel like I'm such a pain in the neck. In fact, people even seem glad to have me around.

This spring, when Dad and Emily and I returned to Birdsong Trail, I took binoculars to watch for eagles. Instead, I spied a pair of ducks in the stream.

A thunderstorm sent us dashing back toward the car. Just as we were rounding the bend by the bird feeder, thunder clapped and lightning nearly blinded us. Dad tripped over a rock and twisted his knee.

His face wrinkled with pain. "Emily, you're the oldest," he said. "Will you follow the trail back to the ranger station and get help?" She looked scared. "I don't know the way...." she began.

"I can find it, Dad!" I interrupted. "After you pass the old gate, you follow this trail till you cross the creek and turn at the signpost with the eagle on it. It's not far to the ranger station after that."

"Ben, I knew those eagle eyes of yours would come in handy," Dad replied. "You'll find the way just fine. Emily can stay here to keep me company."

As I turned to go, Dad called, "Hurry, Ben! I need you."

Swift as an eagle, I zoomed off toward the ranger station and got help for Dad. I was the only one who could do it.

And that's when I realized it's good to be me.

PARENT RESOURCE GUIDE

New vistas on Attention Deficit Disorder (ADD)

In November 1990, parents of children with ADD heaved a collective sigh of relief when Dr. Alan Zametkin released a report that hyperactivity (which is closely linked to ADD) results from an insufficient rate of glucose metabolism in the brain. Finally, commented a supporter, we have an answer to skeptics who pass this off as bratty behavior caused by poor parenting.

We parents have no choice but to deal with our youngsters' ADD, because their behaviors cry out to us for a response. Each time we see a typical ADD problem—losing personal belongings, speaking out of turn, or failing to follow through on responsibilities—we have to make a choice about our reaction. Do we diminish our children with angry criticism or work with them so the situations don't arise again?

Here are several things our family has done to help life run more smoothly with our ADD child. I hope they work for you, too.

1) Learn all you can about how ADD affects people from childhood through adulthood. Use the resources listed in this book; get counseling to identify specific ways your child can adjust; join a support group to swap stories with other parents.

2) Restructure your home environment to accommodate your ADD child. She'll be less distracted when you follow a daily schedule, as we do with the "Morning Song" to help our children get ready for school. Reduce the clutter in your child's room by helping her sort belongings into their assigned places. Choose closed boxes rather than open bins and soothing colors instead of busy wallpaper.

3) Support your child's teacher by telling her about his strengths and weaknesses and by lending her books or videos from the resource list. Ask her to seat him near her desk; to stand next to him when giving directions; to help him keep his workspace organized; and to shorten homework assignments when he becomes overwhelmed (just the odd numbers in math, rather than all the problems, for example). Empty his backpack frequently and follow through on notes he forgets to bring to your attention.

4)   Consider medication, if recommended by your child's physician. The right prescription can help your ADD youngster settle down long enough to benefit from the other steps I've outlined. However, medication *should never be considered a substitute* for the necessary changes at home and at school.

5)   Experiment with ways to calm your child and help her focus. You can often soothe a youngster who fidgets by rubbing her back softly in a circular motion. If she has trouble going to sleep, let her turn on a fan or listen to instrumental music designed for meditation and relaxation. A backrub or foot rub before bed can finish the day on a friendly note.

6)   Schedule regular times for your personal self-renewal, and consider some of the following activities: worship; giving or receiving a massage; meditation and/or yoga; exercise or sports; taking a class; taking a walk or a leisurely bath; going to the library; going on "dates" with a friend or spouse; "adults-only" dinners at home, spending time on your hobby, etc. If you feel guilty about devoting time to yourself, remind yourself that the peace and perspective you gain from such pursuits will spill over into family life and everyone else will benefit, too.

Feel overwhelmed? You probably will be if you try to maintain a "normal" family life that includes hours of TV and a dizzying round of after-school activities, social obligations, and committees. Our family is happier when we concentrate on the essentials—academics and work, family time, and periods of self-renewal. After we've met these needs, we add small doses of the "extras". It's a constant juggling act, but worth the effort. Because of this structure, all of us seem to have a stronger sense of who we are, what we want, and how we're going to get it.

—Jeanne Gehret, 1991

PARENT RESOURCE GUIDE

A quick overview of Attention Deficit Disorder

The symptoms—with and without hyperactivity

Attention Deficit Disorder can be present with or without hyperactivity. The behaviors listed below are commonly attributed to Attention Deficit Disorder with Hyperactivity (ADHD). The affected child will have at least eight of the following characteristics before the age of seven:

- difficulty sitting still; feeling restless
- distractibility
- tendency to get out of classroom seat
- difficulty waiting for a turn
- blurting out answers even before questions or instructions are completed
- impulsivity
- switching from one task to another without completing any
- talking too much
- interrupting
- losing or forgetting things
- failing to notice how others feel

When hyperactivity is not present, the primary symptoms are failure to pay attention, difficulty staying organized, and acting quiet or withdrawn. Children who have ADD without hyperactivity are often overlooked because they are not noisy or overactive.

Prevalence through the lifespan

Estimates on ADD range from 3 percent to 5 percent of the U.S. population (between 1.4 and 2.2 million), with boys outnumbering girls.

In about one-third of children with ADD, symptoms persist into adulthood, although excessive activity may cease to be a problem. Adults with ADD often report that they have trouble establishing and keeping relationships, staying organized, or holding a steady job. They may find it difficult to concentrate for a long time and need frequent changes in their lives. However, adults with ADD often have great success in creative careers that require them to see many perspectives at once; have high energy; perform multiple tasks simultaneously; and launch new projects.

Selected resources on Attention Deficit Disorder and learning differences

For students:
- Matthew Galvin, *Otto Learns About His Medicine.* Magination Press. Ages 6 to 10.
- Jeanne Gehret, *The Don't-give-up-Kid and Learning Differences.* Verbal Images Press, 19 Fox Hill Drive, Fairport, NY 14450. Ages 6 to 10.
- Mel Levine, M.D., *Keeping A Head in School: A Student's Book about Learning Abilities and Learning Disorders.* Educators Publishing Service, Inc. Ages 10 and up.

For adults:
- Nathan H. Azrin and Victoria A. Besalel, *Parents Guide to Bedwetting Control: A Step-by-Step Method.* Pocket Books.
- Melody Beattie, *Codependent No More: How to Stop Controlling Others and Start Caring for Yourself.* Harper and Row.
- Mary Cahill Fowler, *Maybe You Know My Kid.* Birch Lane Press.
- Ronald J. Friedman and Guy T. Doyal, *Attention Deficit Disorder and Hyperactivity.* Pro-Ed, 8700 Shoal Creek Boulevard, Austin, TX 78758.
- Barry Garfinkel, *What is Attention Deficit and How Does Medication Help?* Division of Child and Adolescent Psychiatry, Box 95 UMN&C, Harvard Street at East River Road, Minneapolis, MN 55455.
- Michael Gordon, Ph.D., *ADHD/Hyperactivity: A Consumer's Guide For Parents & Teachers.* GSI Publications, PO Box 746, DeWitt, NY 13214.
- Richard Lavoie, "How Difficult Can This Be?" (video to simulate the feelings of a child with learning or attention problems) PBS Video, 1320 Braddock Place, Alexandria, VA 22314.
- Betty Osman, *No One to Play With: The Social Side of Learning Disabilities.* Academic Therapy Publications.
- Harvey C. Parker, *The ADD Hyperactivity Workbook for Parents, Teachers, and Kids.* Impact Publications, 300 NW 70th Ave., Plantation, FL 33317.
- John Taylor, *Helping Your Hyperactive Child.* SUN Books, 5406 Battlecreek Road SE, Salem, OR 97306.
- G. Weiss and L. Hechtman, *Hyperactive Children Grown-Up.* Guilford Publications.
- CH.A.D.D. newsletter (available with membership from CH.A.D.D.), 499 NW 70th Ave., Suite 308, Plantation, FL, 33317.
- CHALLENGE, Inc. newsletter (about ADD), PO Box 2001, West Newbury, MA 01985.

About the author

In *Eagle Eyes,* Jeanne Gehret draws deeply from her teaching and parenting experiences and her love for the outdoors. Before writing books, she wrote many articles on natural history and was the education reporter for a large school district, where she won writing and photography awards. Since the 1990 release of her book *The Don't-give-up Kid,* she has lectured and networked widely on behalf of children with unique learning styles.

About the illustrator

From her youth, Susan Covert has captured the beauty of nature's changing scenes in her sketchbook. After earning her BFA from Washington University, she became a freelance illustrator with a special interest in children's issues. A member of the Graphic Artist Guild, she has exhibited many times and won a 1986 CASE Award for her poster on childhood cancer. She has also recently illustrated *Stress Management for Children: A Guide for Parents.*

Works by Jeanne Gehret

Eagle Eyes: A Child's Guide to Paying Attention, 1991, second edition. Ages 6 to 10. 40-page picture book with newly-revised parent resource guide. Hardcover or paperback.

The Don't-give-up Kid and Learning Differences, 1990, second edition. Ages 6 to10. 40-page picture book with newly-revised parent resource guide. Hardcover or paperback.

Watch for new titles in 1992 and beyond.

For a book brochure with complete ordering information, check below.

Looking for a speaker? Check below to receive a brochure entitled "Unforgettable Author Visits".
Jeanne Gehret, guest of dozens of radio and TV shows, has brought her message of hope and practical advice to students, teachers, librarians, and parents nationwide.

Please send me more information:

_____ Book brochure on *Eagle Eyes* and *The Don't-give-up Kid*
_____ Brochure on new books
_____ Quantity discounts
_____ Author visit brochure

Name _____

Street _____

City, state, zip _____

Verbal Images Press
19 Fox Hill Drive • Fairport, New York 14450
(716) 377-3807 • Fax (716) 377-5401